My City Tree Cares for Me

My City Tree Cares for Me

written by
Margaret Hall Spencer

illustrated by Gail Yerrill

LUCIDBOOKS

My City Tree Cares for Me

Published by Lucid Books in Brenham, TX.
www.LucidBooks.net

First Printing 2011

ISBN-13: 9781935909163
ISBN-10: 1-935909-16-9

Special Sales: Most Lucid Books titles are available in special quantity discounts. Custom imprinting or excerpting can also be done to fit special needs. Contact Lucid Books at info@ lucidbooks.net.

Note:
The Tree City USA program, sponsored by the Arbor Day Foundation in cooperation with the USDA Forest Service and the National Association of State Foresters, provides direction, technical assistance, public attention, and national recognition for urban and community forestry programs in thousands of towns and cities that more than 135 million Americans call home. Tree City USA is a registered trademark of the Arbor Day Foundation.

Dedication

God causes all things to work together for our good.
Romans 8:28

For Robin, who loves, supports and encourages me every day.
You are my sunshine.

Thank you Debbie, Lee, Shirley, and Todd.
I cherish my friendship with each of you.

Callie looked out the window from the back seat of the car as her family got close to the new town where they were moving.

She didn't know if she would be happy living in the city. She would miss all the fun things she loved about the country.

As they got to the city limits, though, she saw a sign that made her feel better right away. The sign said "Welcome. We are a Tree City USA®." "Trees in a city?" thought Callie. "When I think about cities, I think about big buildings and pavement and lots of traffic on busy streets. I don't think about trees."

Then Callie's eyes grew wide as she saw trees growing along the sides of the streets and a park with trees everywhere. There were even trees around the parking lot at the local shopping center!

The best thing of all was the big, beautiful tree she saw in the front yard when they turned into a driveway and her dad said, "This is it. This is our new home!"

As her mom and dad went inside to unpack boxes, Callie ran through her new front yard to get a closer look at the tree. It was gigantic – so big that she couldn't get her arms around it – so tall that she couldn't even see the bird she heard singing from the top of it! The leaves were so large that just one could cover her entire hand! Callie knew that there was something very special about this tree.

The trip had been long, the afternoon was warm, and Callie felt tired as she sat in the shade of her tree. A little while later, Callie realized she had been sleeping when she heard a voice softly saying, "Hello." She looked around, but didn't see anyone. "Hello," she heard again, and then she realized…it was her tree!

"Hello tree," she replied, "I'm Callie and my parents and I just moved here."

"It's nice to meet you, Callie. I'm Baxter and I'm a bur oak tree. I'm glad that my shade kept you comfortable while you took a nap."

"It did! Thank you!" said Callie. "You are magnificent! Please tell me all about yourself."

"Well," said Baxter, "bur oaks are one of the biggest kinds of oak trees. We can grow to 70 feet tall. That's as tall as the seven-story office building here in the city. As you can see, my bark is rough and my acorns and leaves are huge."

Baxter continued, "I've been here for 20 years, so I'm not full-grown yet. The people who lived here before you planted me when I was just a little guy, and the way this town and its citizens take care of us trees, I'll be here for a long, long time. We bur oaks can live for hundreds of years, you know."

"I have so many questions," said Callie. "Why does this city love its trees so much? Why did the people who lived here before me pick this spot to plant you when you were a little guy?"

Baxter replied, "I'll tell you why I was chosen. Then I'll get a friend of mine to show you around town and tell you about the other trees and why the city loves them. How does that sound?"

"That sounds fun!" replied Callie.

"The people chose a bur oak and picked this spot for me for a few reasons. The yard here is big, so they wanted a tree that would get big. They liked wildlife, and my acorns provide food while my size makes a nice, safe place for birds to nest – or just sit and sing for a while. You've already enjoyed one of the best things I provide, shade. They planted me here on the west side of the house so my shade keeps the house cooler in the summertime. Then when winter comes and I lose my leaves, the sun can shine in and make the house warm."

"Wow! That's interesting!" said Callie. "Now I'm ready to learn about the other trees around town.

"Okay," said Baxter, "meet my friend, Mac."

From one of Baxter's limbs, down came the biggest acorn Callie had ever seen.

"Hi there Callie, I'm Mac. It's nice to meet you! Let's head to the park."

"Let's go," said Callie.

"The smart people in this city know that trees aren't just beautiful, but that they also do a lot of good things," said Mac.

"Baxter told me about the shade and the wildlife. What other good things do city trees do?" asked Callie.

"A lot of things," replied Mac. "Look in the park and notice how many families and friends are there. Just being around trees makes people feel better. A lot of those people didn't know each other and now they are friends because they enjoy being at the park around the trees."

"There are trees along the streets because the people who work at the city know that the leaves keep rain water from rushing down the storm drains so fast. This helps prevent flooding. They know that the shade helps the pavement on the street last longer, too."

"There are trees around the parking lots at our shopping centers and businesses because people like shopping at a place with trees better than shopping at a place with just a plain old paved parking lot. The business owners know this and want the trees there to attract more customers.

All those trees combined really make the parking lot cooler in the summertime, too. Guess how much cooler, Callie?"

"Hmmm," Callie thought about it. "Is it 5 degrees cooler?"

"That's a good answer and that's about how much cooler Baxter makes your front yard all by himself," replied Mac. "All these trees together at this parking lot, though, can make it up to 14 degrees cooler."

"That's amazing!" said Callie.

"Trees are amazing," said Mac. "Their leaves also make use of the pollution that comes out of cars. It's called carbon dioxide and the leaves take it in and combine it with the energy from sunshine to make the food the tree needs. The leaves then release oxygen. So they are cleaning the air we breathe, and that's very important in a city with lots of cars and buses."

"Let's go back to my house and talk to Baxter," said Callie. "I can't wait to tell him what I've learned."

"Baxter, Baxter," Callie called as she and Mac got back to her front yard, "Mac is so smart and he told me how important trees are in a city."

"I'm glad you enjoyed the tour, Callie," replied Baxter. "We are lucky to be in a city that recognizes all the good things trees do. The city has rules that protect us from being damaged when there is construction going on, and people that prune some of us if a limb gets too low or breaks. They have a plan and know where new trees are needed and what kind of trees to plant. They even have a day every year when they celebrate us. It's called Arbor Day. The city and the residents who live here take care of us because they know we take care of them."

Callie noticed that the afternoon sun was going away and the evening birds were singing from Baxter's limbs.

"Baxter and Mac," Callie said, "I'm going in for dinner and telling my parents why trees are very important now that we live in the city. I'm so happy that I live here and that you are in my yard."

"Goodnight," said Baxter. "Goodnight," said Mac. "We'll see you tomorrow."

"Hey, guys," called Callie, "Thank you for taking care of me."

*J*ust think how nice the world
would be if every
city loved
its trees.

About the Author

Margaret Hall Spencer received her horticultural and arboricultural education from the Texas A&M University System. She is a Certified Arborist & Municipal Specialist with expertise in the extra care and planning needed for trees in urban areas. She is a member of the International Society of Arboriculture, Society of Municipal Arborists and serves on the Board of Directors for the Houston Area Urban Forestry Council. Margaret is a landscape and arboricultural consultant and owner of Streamside Green, LLC. She lives in the Houston area with her husband, Robin, and their two dogs and cat Angel, Xena and Albert. She enjoys traveling, photography, music, public speaking and teaching people about trees.

www.ingramcontent.com/pod-product-compliance
Lightning Source LLC
Chambersburg PA
CBHW060828270326
41931CB00002B/97